SCHOLASTIC

Reading Passages
That Build Comprehension

MAIN IDEA & DETAILS

BY LINDA WARD BEECH

NEW YORK • TORONTO • LONDON • AUCKLAND • SYDNEY
MEXICO CITY • NEW DELHI • HONG KONG • BUENOS AIRES

Teaching *Resources*

Contents

Cover design by Maria Lilja
Interior design by Holly Grundon
Interior art by Mike Gordon

ISBN 0-439-55425-X
Copyright © 2005 by Linda Ward Beech.
All rights reserved.
Printed in the U.S.A.

1 2 3 4 5 6 7 8 9 10   40   14 13 12 11 10 09 08 07 06 05

Introduction

Reading comprehension involves numerous thinking skills. Identifying main ideas and the details that support them is one such skill. A reader who is adept at identifying main ideas makes better sense of a text and increases his or her comprehension of what is being communicated. This book will help you help students learn to recognize main ideas and the details that develop them. Use the pages that follow to teach this skill to students and to give them practice in employing it.

Using This Book

Pages 5–7

After introducing main ideas and supporting details to students (see page 4), duplicate and pass out pages 5–7. Use page 5 to help students review and practice what they have just learned about identifying the main idea and supporting details. By explaining their thinking, students are using metacognition to analyze how they recognized main ideas. Pages 6–7 give students a model of the practice pages to come. They also provide a model of the thinking students might use in choosing the best words to represent a main idea or supporting detail from the paragraph.

Page 8

Use this page as a pre-assessment to find out how students think when they identify main ideas. When going over these pages with students, discuss why some choices represent main ideas and why some represent information in the passage but do not state the main idea.

Pages 9–43

These pages offer practice in identifying main ideas and supporting details. The first question asks students to identify the main idea, while the second question requires students to focus on supporting details. The third question asks students to revisit the main idea by choosing the best title for the paragraph. Be sure students understand that the title should summarize the main idea. After reading the paragraph, students should fill in the bubble in front of the correct answer for each question.

Pages 44–46

After they have completed the practice pages, use these pages to assess the way students think when they identify main ideas and supporting details. Explain that for the first exercise students should circle the main idea sentence in the paragraph and then write their own title that summarizes the main idea. The second exercise asks students to circle the main idea and to cross out a sentence in the paragraph that is not a detail.

Page 47

You may wish to keep a record of students' progress as they complete the practice pages. Sample comments that will help you guide students toward improving their skills might include:

- reads carelessly
- misunderstands text
- doesn't recognize main ideas
- has trouble differentiating main ideas from supporting details

Teacher Tip

For students who need extra help, you might suggest that they keep pages 5–7 with them to use as examples when they complete the practice pages.

Mini-Lesson: Teaching About Main Idea & Details

1. Introduce the concept: Write these words on the chalkboard:

gray   pink   lime   colors   tan   purple

Ask students which of the words tells what all the words are about.

2. Model thinking: After students have correctly identified *colors* as the word that tells what the other words are about, explore why they chose this answer by modeling how they might think aloud.

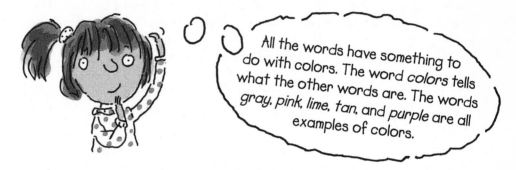

All the words have something to do with colors. The word *colors* tells what the other words are. The words *gray, pink, lime, tan,* and *purple* are all examples of colors.

3. Define the skill: Remind students that when they read a paragraph, the sentences in it are related to one another. The sentences are all about a **main idea.** This is the key point in the paragraph, just as *colors* is the key word in the example on the chalkboard. Explain that very often the main idea is stated in the first sentence of a paragraph. However, the main idea can also be given in the middle or at the end of a paragraph.

Tell students that the other sentences in a paragraph tell more about the main idea. These sentences give **supporting details**. A supporting detail might be an example such as the color words on the chalkboard. A supporting detail might also be a fact about the main idea or a description of it. Explain that supporting details fill in information about the main idea and make the paragraph more interesting to read. Help students understand that the main idea is bigger or broader than the supporting details.

Use graphic organizers such as the examples shown here to help students who are visual learners understand the concept.

4. Practice the skill: Use Practice Pages 9–43 to give students practice in identifying main idea and supporting details.

Example 1

Main Idea

Detail   Detail   Detail

Example 2

I. Main Idea
   A. Detail
   B. Detail
   C. Detail

Name_____ Date_____

What Is a Main Idea?
What Are Supporting Details?

You read a paragraph. It might give you a lot of information. A lot of information can be confusing. How does a reader handle this? A good reader sorts out the information. A reader might think:

What is the main point of this paragraph?

What other information is given? How does it help me understand the main point?

When you answer the first question, you identify the **main idea**. The main idea is what the paragraph is about. When you answer the other questions, you identify the details. The **details** support or tell more about the main idea.

Read the paragraph below, and then complete each sentence.

Dolphins are good learners. They learn to play games. They learn to do tricks. Trainers have taught dolphins how to save lives. One trainer even taught his dolphins to clean out their tank. For each piece of trash they brought him, he gave them a fish.

1. This paragraph is mainly about

_____.

2. One detail about the main idea is

_____.

3. Another detail about the main idea is

_____.

4. The details help me understand the main idea because they

_____.

5. The main idea is in the _____ sentence.

Name _____   Date _____

Identifying Main Idea & Supporting Details

Study these two pages. They show how a student
identified the main idea and supporting details.

Read the paragraph. Then fill in the
bubble that best completes each sentence.

The first U.S. zoo opened in Philadelphia in 1874. Visitors were thrilled to see animals from all over the world. The zoo had six giraffes, an elephant named Jennie, and many colorful birds. It also had some animals from Australia. People were amazed at the kangaroos, wombats, and dingoes.

---

1. The main idea of the paragraph is

○ A. the different animals
     from Australia

○ C. how people felt at seeing
     strange animals

The paragraph tells about animals from Australia, but it tells about other animals too.

Some sentences tell how people felt, but most of the sentences are about the zoo.

● B. the first zoo in the
     United States

This is what the first sentence says. The other sentences all tell about this zoo.

I am going to fill in B. This sentence seems to be the main point of the paragraph. The other sentences tell more about it.

Continued ⟶

Identifying Main Idea & Supporting Details
(Continued)

2. A detail that tells about the main idea is

○ A. the American animals thrilled visitors

> The paragraph says the animals are from all over the world, not just the U.S.

● C. the zoo had some animals from Australia

> The zoo did have animals from Australia. It even gives some examples.

○ B. the visitors came from all over the world

> It doesn't say the visitors are from all over the world. I think the visitors were probably Americans, mostly from Philadelphia.

> I am going to fill in **C.** This sentence gives more information about the first zoo; the others do not.

3. The best title for this paragraph would be

● A. America's First Zoo

> This title tells about the whole paragraph.

○ C. An Elephant Named Jennie

> This title only tells about part of the paragraph.

○ B. Welcome to Philadelphia

> This title doesn't tell about the zoo.

> I am going to fill in **A.** It sums up what the paragraph is all about.

Name_____ Date_____

Sorting Information

Read each paragraph. Write **main idea** or **detail** next to each group of words.

1. Patricia Polacco often writes books that recall her childhood. *Chicken Sunday* is based on some neighbors. The books *Thundercake* and *Meteor* take place on her grandparents' farm.

   A. _____ neighbors

   B. _____ books about Polacco's childhood

   C. _____ grandparents' farm

2. Did you know that Orange is in Texas? Have you heard of Bacon, Georgia? Some towns are named for food.

   A. _____ food names for towns

   B. _____ Orange

   C. _____ Bacon

3. You might see animals in an African jungle. You might ride the big waves in a pool. You can visit the future too. Theme parks offer many different thrills.

   A. _____ big waves

   B. _____ the future

   C. _____ theme park thrills

4. San Francisco is known for many things. It has cable cars on its steep hills. It is famous for a chocolate candy. People also like its sourdough bread.

   A. _____ famous San Francisco things

   B. _____ chocolate

   C. _____ cable cars

Practice Page 1

Name_____   Date_____

Read the paragraph. Then fill in the bubble that best completes each sentence.

Mount Rushmore is a huge carving in a stone cliff. The carving shows the faces of four U.S. presidents. They are George Washington, Thomas Jefferson, Theodore Roosevelt, and Abraham Lincoln. Mount Rushmore is in South Dakota. Each year many people visit this amazing sight.

1. **The main idea of the paragraph is**

   ○ A. what Mount Rushmore is

   ○ B. where Mount Rushmore is

   ○ C. the names of the presidents

2. **A detail that tells about the main idea is**

   ○ A. how the four presidents were chosen

   ○ B. which presidents are at Mount Rushmore

   ○ C. why Mount Rushmore is in South Dakota

3. **The best title for this paragraph would be**

   ○ A. The Face of Washington

   ○ B. Visiting South Dakota

   ○ C. Mount Rushmore Carvings

Practice Page **2**

Name_____ Date_____

Read the paragraph. Then fill in the bubble that best completes each sentence.

Crows are the robbers of the bird world. Crows especially like to steal food from other birds. Sometimes they are very bold about taking things. They might chase another bird, cackle at it, or even bump into it. At other times crows are sneaky. They get close and then snatch food away when another bird isn't looking.

1. **The main idea of the paragraph is**
   - A. why crows like to take food
   - B. the kind of food that crows eat
   - C. how crows act like thieves

2. **A detail that tells about the main idea is**
   - A. how crows can be sneaky
   - B. how other birds fight crows
   - C. where crows make their nests

3. **The best title for this paragraph would be**
   - A. A Bump from a Crow
   - B. Bandit Birds
   - C. What Crows Eat

Practice Page **3**

Name_____ Date_____

Read the paragraph. Then fill in the bubble that best completes each sentence.

The year was 1850. The place was New York City. A gentleman was on his way to a wedding. He was all dressed up. However, it had just rained, and the streets were muddy. The man turned up the bottoms of his pants to keep them clean. At the wedding, he forgot to turn them down. That is how the fashion for cuffs on pants got started.

1. **The main idea of the paragraph is**

   ○ A. what New York was like in 1850

   ○ B. the story behind cuffs on pants

   ○ C. how to keep pants clean in the mud

2. **A detail that tells about the main idea is**

   ○ A. why the man turned up his pants

   ○ B. who was getting married that day

   ○ C. what people said about the weather

3. **The best title for this paragraph would be**

   ○ A. A Rainy Day in New York

   ○ B. Keeping Your Clothes Clean

   ○ C. How Cuffs Turned Up

Practice Page 4

Name_____ Date_____

Read the paragraph. Then fill in the bubble that best completes each sentence.

It takes a lot of trucks to get an airplane ready to fly. Fuel trucks are very important. They fill the fuel tanks of planes. Baggage trucks carry people's suitcases to and from planes. Still other trucks deliver food. You might also see mail trucks and cargo trucks. Also standing by at airports are repair trucks.

1. **The main idea of the paragraph is**

   ○ A. airplanes are like trucks

   ○ B. some trucks carry food

   ○ C. how trucks help planes

2. **A detail that tells about the main idea is**

   ○ A. trucks are more important than planes

   ○ B. many people carry on their luggage

   ○ C. airplanes depend on trucks for fuel

3. **The best title for this paragraph would be**

   ○ A. The Role of Trucks at Airports

   ○ B. Repair Trucks on the Runway

   ○ C. Mail Trucks and Cargo Trucks

Practice Page 5

Name_____ Date_____

Read the paragraph. Then fill in the bubble that best completes each sentence.

A mericans like toast, eggs, and cereal. In China people eat congee, a thick rice. People in Japan often have a soup called miso. Pancakes made from lentil beans are favored in India. Bread and coffee with milk are the most popular breakfast foods in France. Breakfast around the world is a matter of different tastes.

1. The main idea of the paragraph is

  ○ A. people in China and Japan like different foods

  ○ B. cereal is a popular breakfast food in the United States

  ○ C. people eat different foods for breakfast around the world

2. A detail that tells about the main idea is

  ○ A. breakfast is an important meal

  ○ B. everyone eats eggs at breakfast

  ○ C. people in India eat lentil pancakes

3. The best title for this paragraph would be

  ○ A. Soup in the Morning

  ○ B. Breakfast Around the World

  ○ C. Something to Eat

Practice Page **6**

Name_____ Date_____

Read the paragraph. Then fill in the bubble that best completes each sentence.

The Holland Tunnel is a roadway under the Hudson River. At one end of the tunnel is New York City. At the other end is the state of New Jersey. Almost 50,000 cars and trucks go through the Holland Tunnel each day. The distance is just over one and a half miles. Depending on the time of day, it can be a long or short trip.

1. The main idea of the paragraph is

  ○ A. what the Holland Tunnel is

  ○ B. the length of the Holland Tunnel

  ○ C. what the Hudson River is like

2. A detail that tells more about the main idea is

  ○ A. the places that the tunnel connects

  ○ B. how to get through the tunnel

  ○ C. other ways to cross the Hudson River

3. The best title for this paragraph would be

  ○ A. A Long or Short Trip

  ○ B. Riding Through a Tunnel

  ○ C. Holland Tunnel Facts

Practice Page 7

Name_____ Date_____

Read the paragraph. Then fill in the bubble that best completes each sentence.

Can you name the planets in our solar system? Mercury is one of them. Like the other planets, Mercury moves in a path around the sun. Mercury travels faster than the other planets. It speeds along at about 107,000 miles an hour. Mercury is the planet closest to the sun. Its days are very hot, and its nights are very cold. There is no water on Mercury.

1. **The main idea of the paragraph is**

   ○ A. the lack of water on Mercury

   ○ B. the planets in the solar system

   ○ C. what the planet Mercury is like

2. **A detail that tells more about the main idea is**

   ○ A. the speed at which Mercury travels around the sun

   ○ B. the names of the other planets in the solar system

   ○ C. how fast other planets in the solar system travel

3. **The best title for this paragraph would be**

   ○ A. Moving Around the Sun

   ○ B. Hot Days and Cold Nights

   ○ C. The Planet Mercury

Name_____   Date_____

Read the paragraph. Then fill in the bubble that best completes each sentence.

Horses are often helpers for humans. In some communities the police ride horses to control large crowds. Cowboys use horses to help round up herds of cattle. In some countries farmers still use horses to pull plows or wagons. People also use horses to carry them from place to place.

1. The main idea of the paragraph is

○ A. the different jobs that horses can do

○ B. how the police use horses in crowds

○ C. the ways that animals help people

2. A detail that tells more about the main idea is

○ A. how cowboys use horses in their work

○ B. the kinds of horses used in police work

○ C. the names of countries using farm horses

3. The best title for this paragraph would be

○ A. Helpful Horses

○ B. Horses in Parades

○ C. Traveling by Horse

Practice Page 9

Name_____ Date_____

Read the paragraph. Then fill in the bubble that best completes each sentence.

Community names often have words for water in them. For example, Riverview is a town in Kansas. Running Springs is in California. You'll find Bay City in Michigan. Storm Lake is in Iowa, Great Falls is in Montana, and Brookfield is in Vermont. Where is Silver Creek? Why, it's in Mississippi.

WELCOME TO RUNNING SPRINGS

1. The main idea of the paragraph is

○ A. where to find Silver Creek

○ B. names of places with water words

○ C. different bodies of water in states

2. A detail that tells more about the main idea is

○ A. which state has the most bodies of water

○ B. in which state you'll find Bay City

○ C. why water words appear in names

3. The best title for this paragraph would be

○ A. Where Is Storm Lake?

○ B. Water Words in Place Names

○ C. How Communities Are Named

Practice Page 10

Name_____ Date_____

Read the paragraph. Then fill in the bubble that best completes each sentence.

What foods cause the most problems in a car? Chocolate is one. It gets all over things. When drivers try to clean up the mess, they often have accidents. Hot drinks such as coffee are also dangerous. Why? They spill. Greasy foods cause trouble when they drip. Jelly doughnuts cause problems too. Can you guess why?

1. **The main idea of the paragraph is**
   - ○ A. foods that are good for car rides
   - ○ B. the problems caused by chocolate
   - ○ C. foods that cause problems in cars

2. **A detail that tells more about the main idea is**
   - ○ A. greasy foods that drip cause problems
   - ○ B. drivers should pay attention to the road
   - ○ C. cell phones are dangerous in cars

3. **The best title for this paragraph would be**
   - ○ A. Chocolate Causes Accidents
   - ○ B. Please Eat Neatly
   - ○ C. Messy Foods in Cars

Practice Page 11

Name_____ Date_____

Read the paragraph. Then fill in the bubble that best completes each sentence.

Many U.S. presidents have had nicknames. James Madison was sometimes called Jemmy. Honest Abe was a popular name for Abraham Lincoln. Dwight Eisenhower was known as Ike, and Theodore Roosevelt was Teddy. Several presidents have been called by their initials. John F. Kennedy was JFK, while Lyndon B. Johnson was LBJ.

1. **The main idea of the paragraph is**
   - ○ A. the nickname of President Eisenhower
   - ○ B. nicknames for some U.S. presidents
   - ○ C. how presidents got their nicknames

2. **A detail that tells more about the main idea is**
   - ○ A. not all U.S. presidents have had nicknames
   - ○ B. some nicknames have come from a president's initials
   - ○ C. only popular presidents have had nicknames

3. **The best title for this paragraph would be**
   - ○ A. Nicknames for Presidents
   - ○ B. Lincoln Was Honest Abe
   - ○ C. Who Was Jemmy?

Name_____ **Date**_____

Read the paragraph. Then fill in the bubble that best completes each sentence.

Do you know what a *chinook* is? It's a warm winter wind in the western United States. Another wind is a *purga*. This very cold wind brings snow to Russia. In France there is a dry wind called a *mistral*. Egypt has a *khamsin*. This wind blows across the desert, stirring up sand. Around the world different winds come and go with the seasons.

1. The main idea of the paragraph is

○ A. winds of the western U.S.

○ B. how winds bring snow to Russia

○ C. different winds around the world

2. A detail that tells more about the main idea is

○ A. what a *purga* is and does

○ B. where the word *mistral* comes from

○ C. how people dress during a *khamsin*

3. The best title for this paragraph would be

○ A. Cold Winter Winds

○ B. What's the Weather?

○ C. Winds of the World

Practice Page **13**

Name_____ Date_____

Read the paragraph. Then fill in the bubble that best completes each sentence.

Beatrix Potter (1866–1943) loved animals. She also loved to draw. As a young girl she kept a sketchbook of plants and family pets. She became a student of nature. Later on Beatrix Potter wrote stories for children. The main characters were animals. Perhaps you have read *The Tale of Peter Rabbit* or *Squirrel Nutkin*.

1. The main idea of the paragraph is

○ A. Beatrix Potter's interest in nature

○ B. the titles of Beatrix Potter's books

○ C. the names of Potter family pets

2. A detail that tells more about the main idea is

○ A. how Beatrix Potter learned to draw

○ B. what Potter drew in her sketchbook

○ C. how the book *Squirrel Nutkin* ends

3. The best title for this paragraph would be

○ A. Meet These Animal Characters

○ B. The Words of Beatrix Potter

○ C. Potter and the Natural World

Practice Page **14**

Name_____ Date_____

Read the paragraph. Then fill in the bubble that best completes each sentence.

People often play with words when they name their boats. Go down to the harbor and you might see a boat named *Knot A Care*. Some other names with double meanings are *Willy Tippit*, *Sea Ya*, and *Reel Time*. Perhaps you will spot the *Crewless* or the *Scuba Due*. Don't leave until it's official. Find the *O-Fish-Hull*!

1. The main idea of the paragraph is

○ A. finding a boat called *Scuba Due*

○ B. boat names with double meanings

○ C. an official visit to the harbor

2. A detail that tells more about the main idea is

○ A. a boat might have a name such as *Sea Ya*

○ B. a popular boat name is *Serenity*

○ C. why people don't name their houses

3. The best title for this paragraph would be

○ A. Fun With Boat Names

○ B. Who Is Willy Tippit?

○ C. Boats in the Harbor

Practice Page 15   Name_____   Date_____

Read the paragraph. Then fill in the bubble that best completes each sentence.

What is a census? A census is a count. Every ten years the U.S. Census Bureau counts people. It also finds out where people live, the kind of work they do, and other facts. The census tells whether the population of a state changes. The number of representatives a state has in Congress depends on its population. Census numbers are helpful in planning new roads, schools, and other things.

1. **The main idea of the paragraph is**

   ○ A. how Congress changes

   ○ B. why populations change

   ○ C. what the census is

2. **A detail that tells more about the main idea is**

   ○ A. how many people now live in the U.S.

   ○ B. which states have the most people

   ○ C. how the census numbers are used

3. **The best title for this paragraph would be**

   ○ A. Every Ten Years

   ○ B. The Census Counts

   ○ C. Where People Live

Practice Page 16

Name_____   Date_____

Read the paragraph. Then fill in the bubble that best completes each sentence.

Goats help prevent fires in California. In parts of the state, the fall season is very dry. Hot winds blow over the land. The smallest spark can start a fire. The fires spread easily through grasses and bushes. So people use goats to eat the plants as a form of fire control. The goats eat anything, even plants with thorns. Many people rent the goats until the rains come and the danger is over.

1. The main idea of the paragraph is

○ A. goats are not very fussy eaters

○ B. goats prevent fires by clearing land

○ C. California's dangerous dry season

2. A detail that tells more about the main idea is

○ A. the goats are rented for the dry season

○ B. cows do not work well for this job

○ C. goats also eat plants people want to keep

3. The best title for this paragraph would be

○ A. California Fire Safety

○ B. Goats as Firefighters

○ C. The Problems of Fall

Practice Page **17**   Name_____   Date_____

Read the paragraph. Then fill in the bubble that best completes each sentence.

People have used many materials to make maps. At first they drew on rocks, wood, or clay. Sometimes they made maps on animal hides. Later mapmakers painted on silk or scratched on metal. On islands in the Pacific Ocean, people made sailing maps from sticks. The sticks were tied together to show the patterns of winds and waves. Tiny shells were added to show where islands were located.

1. **The main idea of the paragraph is**
   - ○ A. using animal hides for early maps
   - ○ B. different materials used for maps
   - ○ C. sailing maps for the Pacific Ocean

2. **A detail that tells more about the main idea is**
   - ○ A. using maps on the Internet
   - ○ B. maps were painted on silk
   - ○ C. how the first globes were made

3. **The best title for this paragraph would be**
   - ○ A. Sailing With a Map
   - ○ B. Sticks and Stones
   - ○ C. Map Materials

Practice Page 18

Name_____   Date_____

Read the paragraph. Then fill in the bubble that best completes each sentence.

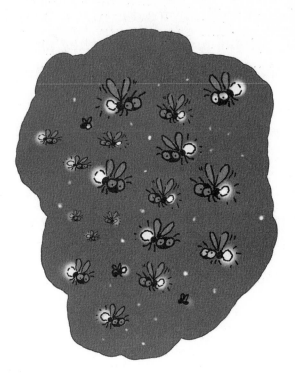

On a summer night you might see the light of a firefly. This light is a mating message to other fireflies. Some ocean creatures also have lights. For example, the light on an angler fish helps it catch food. Other sea creatures with glow lights include jellyfish and shrimp. On land there are glow-in-the-dark creatures such as earthworms. Many kinds of animals have built-in lights.

1. The main idea of the paragraph is

  ○ A. the lights of summer nights

  ○ B. creatures with built-in lights

  ○ C. lights in the deep, dark sea

2. A detail that tells more about the main idea is

  ○ A. how light helps an angler fish

  ○ B. the codes that fireflies use

  ○ C. how animals uses senses at night

3. The best title for this paragraph would be

  ○ A. The Story of Light

  ○ B. Ocean Glow

  ○ C. Creatures of Light

Practice Page 19

Name_____ Date_____

Read the paragraph. Then fill in the bubble that best completes each sentence.

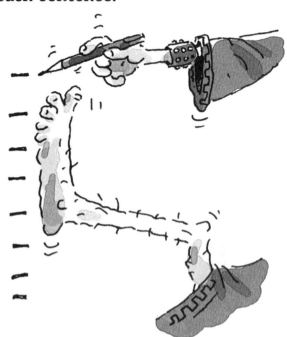

In ancient Rome people used their bodies as measuring tools. They used the length of their foot to measure distance. For smaller lengths they used their thumb. A foot was divided into 12 thumb widths. Today we call these units inches. The Romans measured long distances in paces. A pace was two steps. A thousand paces was called a mille. Today we call this distance a mile.

1. The main idea of the paragraph is

○ A. measurements of ancient Rome

○ B. how inches were once measured

○ C. why Romans used feet to measure

2. A detail that tells more about the main idea is

○ A. how people once measured a yard

○ B. how rulers were first developed

○ C. how the Romans measured a mile

3. The best title for this paragraph would be

○ A. How We Got the Modern Mile

○ B. Measuring from Head to Toe

○ C. The Roman Way of Measuring

Practice Page **20**

Name_____ Date_____

Read the paragraph. Then fill in the bubble that best completes each sentence.

Have you ever played Monopoly? This famous game was invented more than 70 years ago. Times were very hard then. Many people were out of work. Charles B. Darrow had lost his job too. He began designing games to earn money. One game was based on getting rich. For many people the game was a dream of better times. It became one of the world's most famous games.

1. **The main idea of the paragraph is**
   - ⃝ A. how and why Monopoly began
   - ⃝ B. the reason Darrow lost his job
   - ⃝ C. how to play the game of Monopoly

2. **A detail that tells more about the main idea is**
   - ⃝ A. what people liked about Monopoly
   - ⃝ B. how many people could play the game
   - ⃝ C. how much Monopoly costs

3. **The best title for this paragraph would be**
   - ⃝ A. Meet Charles Darrow
   - ⃝ B. The Monopoly Story
   - ⃝ C. Popular Board Games

Name_____ Date_____

Read the paragraph. Then fill in the bubble that best completes each sentence.

Marc Brown writes books about an aardvark named Arthur. Many of Brown's characters are based on people in his life. For example, Buster is based on a childhood friend. So is the character Sue Ellen. Two other characters, D.W. and Francine, are like his sisters in many ways. Another book character is Grandma Thora. She is named for Marc Brown's real grandmother.

1. **The main idea of the paragraph is**

   ○ A. how Marc Brown started writing the Arthur books

   ○ B. why Marc Brown's books have so many characters

   ○ C. where Marc Brown's characters come from

2. **A detail that tells more about the main idea is**

   ○ A. who Francine is based on

   ○ B. why Arthur is an aardvark

   ○ C. where Marc Brown grew up

3. **The best title for this paragraph would be**

   ○ A. The Characters of Marc Brown

   ○ B. Who Is Marc Brown?

   ○ C. Meet the Real Grandma Thora

Practice Page 22

Name_____ Date_____

Read the paragraph. Then fill in the bubble that best completes each question.

Do you know what a palindrome is? It is a word, phrase, or sentence that reads forward or backward the same way. For example, the word M-O-M is a palindrome. Whichever way you read it, it is the same. Other palindrome words are *noon*, *did*, *level*, and *bob*. A famous palindrome sentence is "Madam, I'm Adam." Can you think of some other palindromes?

1. The main idea of the paragraph is

○ A. palindromes as sentences

○ B. words with the same letters

○ C. what a palindrome is

2. A detail that tells more about the main idea is

○ A. what most palindromes mean

○ B. examples of palindrome words

○ C. reading words upside down

3. The best title for this paragraph would be

○ A. Learning About Palindromes

○ B. Some Famous Palindromes

○ C. Going Backward and Forward

Practice Page 23   Name_____   Date_____

Read the paragraph. Then fill in the bubble that best completes each sentence.

Many popular sayings are about dogs. Have you ever been "in the doghouse"? That means you are in trouble. If you are "sick as a dog," you don't feel very well. If you are "dog-tired," you are really weary. Someone who is the "top dog" is the one in charge. What do people say when it is raining very hard? They often claim that it is "raining cats and dogs."

1. **The main idea of the paragraph is**

   ○ A. common sayings with *dog* in them

   ○ B. how people think about dogs and cats

   ○ C. what it is like to be "sick as a dog"

2. **A detail that tells more about the main idea is**

   ○ A. why people use *dog* in many sayings

   ○ B. the meaning of "in the doghouse"

   ○ C. how people feel about dogs as pets

3. **The best title for this paragraph would be**

   ○ A. How to Be a Top Dog

   ○ B. Colorful Sayings Using *Dog*

   ○ C. The Story Behind "Dog-Tired"

Practice Page **24**

Name_____ Date_____

Read the paragraph. Then fill in the bubble that best completes each sentence.

An oyster lies on the warm sea floor. One day a speck of something gets inside the oyster shell. To protect itself, the oyster builds layers of a special material around the speck. The material is called nacre. After a few years a pearl is formed from the nacre. Someday a diver may find this natural pearl. It might become part of a valuable piece of jewelry.

1. The main idea of the paragraph is

○ A. how pearl divers work

○ B. how a pearl is formed

○ C. what the material nacre is

2. A detail that tells more about the main idea is

○ A. how natural pearls differ from cultured ones

○ B. the names of the seas where natural pearls are found

○ C. the role of nacre in forming a natural pearl

3. The best title for this paragraph would be

○ A. How Natural Pearls Are Made

○ B. An Oyster's Life in the Sea

○ C. Using Pearls in Fine Jewelry

Practice Page 25

Name_____ Date_____

Read the paragraph. Then fill in the bubble that best completes each sentence.

Some people think your handwriting tells something about you. They say that up-and-down writing shows a calm, logical person. Is that you? Writing that slants a little to the right means someone is outgoing. If writing slants a lot to the right, that person is very friendly. What about writing that slants to the left? Someone who writes this way is rather quiet.

handwriting

handwriting

handwriting

handwriting

1. **The main idea of the paragraph is**
   - ○ A. why people slant their handwriting
   - ○ B. how friendly, outgoing people write
   - ○ C. what handwriting tells about people

2. **A detail that tells more about the main idea is**
   - ○ A. what kinds of pens people use
   - ○ B. what up-and-down writing means
   - ○ C. how computers have changed writing

3. **The best title for this paragraph would be**
   - ○ A. Writing to the Right
   - ○ B. How to Become a Writer
   - ○ C. The Meaning of Handwriting

Name_____ Date_____

Read the paragraph. Then fill in the bubble that best completes each sentence.

People play chess all over the world. In a town in Italy people are the chess pieces. Every two years the town holds a human chess game. It is played on a huge chessboard painted in the town square. Some players such as the knights ride horses. All are in costumes to look like real chess pieces. Town officials call out the moves as large crowds of people cheer.

1. **The main idea of the paragraph is**
   - ○ A. playing chess with people as pieces
   - ○ B. a town square becomes a chessboard
   - ○ C. how people play chess around the world

2. **A detail that tells more about the main idea is**
   - ○ A. how this human chess game got started
   - ○ B. people who are knights are on horses
   - ○ C. the history of the game of chess

3. **The best title for this paragraph would be**
   - ○ A. Human Chess Pieces
   - ○ B. Costumes for Chess
   - ○ C. Places to See in Italy

Practice Page **27**

Name_____ Date_____

Read the paragraph. Then fill in the bubble that best completes each sentence.

The earliest people did not have a written language. Instead, people learned things by telling and listening to stories. How did storytellers recall everything? Some drew pictures on cave walls to help them remember. Some made up chants to the rhythm of drums. Other storytellers made belts or necklaces. Colored threads, beads, and special knots stood for different events.

1. **The main idea of the paragraph is**
   - ○ A. long-ago drawings on cave walls
   - ○ B. why there were no books or magazines
   - ○ C. different ways storytellers recalled events

2. **A detail that tells more about the main idea is**
   - ○ A. which people became storytellers
   - ○ B. beads on belts helped recall things
   - ○ C. what kinds of stories people told

3. **The best title for this paragraph would be**
   - ○ A. Stories on Television
   - ○ B. Remembering Stories Long Ago
   - ○ C. Using Special Knots

Practice Page **28**

Name_____ Date_____

Read the paragraph. Then fill in the bubble that best completes each sentence.

Dolphins usually work together as a team. They like to travel in groups. Large groups are called herds. Smaller groups are known as pods. If a dolphin is sick, others in the pod will swim alongside of it. They help the sick dolphin get to the water's surface so it can breathe. Dolphins also work together to find food. And when a mother dolphin looks for food, others will care for its baby.

1. The main idea of the paragraph is

○ A. how dolphins work together

○ B. helping out mother dolphins

○ C. how dolphins act with people

2. A detail that tells more about the main idea is

○ A. what dolphins do at school

○ B. different kinds of dolphins

○ C. how dolphins travel in groups

3. The best title for this paragraph would be

○ A. The Teamwork of Dolphins

○ B. Helping a Sick Dolphin

○ C. What Dolphins Look Like

Practice Page 29

Name_____ Date_____

Read the paragraph. Then fill in the bubble that best completes each sentence.

Some people in Asia live in round tents called yurts. A yurt has a wooden frame that is covered with felt. A yurt is good in the wind. Its round shape causes winds to blow around and away from it. The felt covering of a yurt keeps out snow and rain. The felt also keeps in heat given off from stoves inside the yurt. A yurt is a comfortable home in the cool highlands of Central Asia.

1. **The main idea of the paragraph is**
   - ○ A. different kinds of homes around the world
   - ○ B. where in Asia people live in tents called yurts
   - ○ C. how a yurt protects people from the weather

2. **A detail that tells more about the main idea is**
   - ○ A. what kind of furniture is in a yurt
   - ○ B. how long it takes to set up a yurt
   - ○ C. how a yurt's shape helps in wind

3. **The best title for this paragraph would be**
   - ○ A. A Yurt's Felt Covering
   - ○ B. Cooking in a Yurt
   - ○ C. Staying Warm in a Yurt

Practice Page **30**

Name_____ Date_____

Read the paragraph. Then fill in the bubble that best completes each sentence.

Where did the dandelion gets its name? Look carefully at the leaves of this plant. They are jagged, or toothlike. Some say the leaves look like the tooth of a lion. In French the phrase *dent de lion* means just that. If you say dent de lion fast, it sounds like *dandelion* in English. As for the yellow flower of a dandelion, some people think it looks like the fluffy mane of a lion!

1. The main idea of the paragraph is

○ A. the yellow flower of the dandelion

○ B. where the word *dandelion* comes from

○ C. why a lion's tooth looks like a leaf

2. A detail that tells more about the main idea is

○ A. why people think dandelions are weeds

○ B. how French words are spoken fast

○ C. what the term *dent de lion* means

3. The best title for this paragraph would be

○ A. Don't Pick the Dandelions

○ B. The Word History of *Dandelion*

○ C. How Lions Became Flowers

Practice Page 31   Name_____   Date_____

Read the paragraph. Then fill in the bubble
that best completes each sentence.

Wisor is a robot. It can do a job that is
difficult and dangerous for people.
Wisor is shaped something like a torpedo.
The robot works underground in New York
City. Wisor crawls through steam pipes to
find cracks and holes. Five cameras help
Wisor make its way through the twists and
turns of the pipes. Once Wisor finds a crack,
it cleans it out and welds it back together.

1. **The main idea of the paragraph is**
   ○ A. five cameras help Wisor
   ○ B. what Wisor is and does
   ○ C. jobs that robots do well

2. **A detail that tells more about the main idea is**
   ○ A. how Wisor got its name
   ○ B. how many miles of pipes are in the city
   ○ C. the robot is shaped like a torpedo

3. **The best title for this paragraph would be**
   ○ A. Under New York City
   ○ B. A Crack in the Pipes
   ○ C. Wisor at Work

Practice Page 32

Name_____ Date_____

Read the paragraph. Then fill in the bubble that best completes each sentence.

Nylon is a kind of plastic. Like other plastics, nylon is made from crude oil. One of the most important uses of nylon is in making clothing. Perhaps you are wearing something made of nylon today. Nylon is also used to make carpets. Where else will you see nylon? It's used in fishing nets and in the small wheels found in gears. A tennis racquet also has nylon strings.

1. **The main idea of the paragraph is**

   ○ A. information about nylon

   ○ B. carpets made from nylon

   ○ C. the different uses of plastic

2. **A detail that tells more about the main idea is**

   ○ A. nylon is used for tennis racquet strings

   ○ B. rayon is also a man-made fabric

   ○ C. racquet frames were once made of wood

3. **The best title for this paragraph would be**

   ○ A. What Are You Wearing?

   ○ B. Looking at Nylon

   ○ C. Nylon Fishing Nets

Name_____ Date_____

Read the paragraph. Then fill in the bubble that best completes each sentence.

Most animals you see in cities are pets. You might also see some squirrels in city parks. But if you visit Thailand, watch out for monkeys. Many wild monkeys moved into the city of Lop Buri. There the monkeys are troublemakers. They go into houses and take things. On the street they snatch bags and eyeglasses. How do people get their things back? They give food to the monkeys.

1. The main idea of the paragraph is
   - ○ A. squirrels live in many city parks
   - ○ B. monkeys in Lop Buri steal eyeglasses
   - ○ C. wild monkeys cause trouble in Lop Buri

2. A detail that tells more about the main idea is
   - ○ A. chipmunks are another wild animal found in cities
   - ○ B. the monkeys in Lop Buri enter people's homes
   - ○ C. Thailand now has fewer forests than it once did

3. The best title for this paragraph would be
   - ○ A. Monkey Trouble
   - ○ B. Unusual City Pets
   - ○ C. The Food Exchange

Practice Page 34

Name_____ Date_____

Read the paragraph. Then fill in the bubble that best completes each sentence.

A family in Virginia plants a field of corn in the pattern of a maze. The pattern for the maze is designed on a computer. Then family members use the maze map to make paths in the field. They plant the corn around the paths. By July the maze is ready for visitors. It covers 15 acres! Visitors enjoy trying to walk through it. If people get lost, they hold up a flag for help.

1. The main idea of the paragraph is

○ A. how computers are used for mazes

○ B. how a cornfield becomes a maze

○ C. why it's fun to walk through a maze

2. A detail that tells more about the main idea is

○ A. mazes have a long history

○ B. some people plant gardens as mazes

○ C. the corn maze is ready in July

3. The best title for this paragraph would be

○ A. Maze in a Cornfield

○ B. Fly a Flag for Help

○ C. How to Plant Corn

Practice Page **35**

Name_____   Date_____

Read the paragraph. Then fill in the bubble that best completes each sentence.

March is a good month to celebrate authors' birthdays. You can begin on March 2. That's the day when Dr. Seuss was born in 1904. March 11 is the birth date of Ezra Jack Keats. Have you ever read his book *The Snowy Day*? On March 12 you can celebrate the birthday of Virginia Hamilton. One of her well-known books is *The People Could Fly: American Black Folktales*.

1. **The main idea of the paragraph is**
   - ○ A. authors with March birthdays
   - ○ B. the birthday of Virginia Hamilton
   - ○ C. favorite children's book authors

2. **A detail that tells more about the main idea is**
   - ○ A. how Dr. Seuss got started writing
   - ○ B. ways to celebrate an author's birthday
   - ○ C. Ezra Jack Keats was born on March 11

3. **The best title for this paragraph would be**
   - ○ A. A Snowy Day in March
   - ○ B. Happy Birthday, Authors
   - ○ C. What to Read in March

Assessment 1

Name_____ Date_____

Read the paragraph. Circle the sentence that tells the main idea.
Then write a title that tells the main idea.

_____

Title

Pens have come a long way over time. The first pens were sticks with sharp points. Long-ago people used them to draw messages on wet clay. The ancient Egyptians made pens from hollow plant stems called reeds. They dipped the reed pens in paint or ink. Later, people used feathers called quills. Fountain pens were invented about 100 years ago. More recently, ballpoints were developed.

Ink

Read the paragraph. Circle the sentence that tells the main idea.
Cross out the sentence that does NOT tell about the main idea.

People use many slang terms when they talk about money. For example, a buck is a dollar bill. If you have two bits, you have a quarter. A ten-dollar bill is sometimes called a sawbuck. A C-note is a hundred-dollar bill. What is a thousand dollars? That's a grand. A lot of people use credit cards instead of cash. And a slang word for all kinds of money is moolah.

Assessment **2**

Name_____ Date_____

Read the paragraph. Circle the sentence that tells the main idea. Then write a title that tells the main idea.

_____
Title

You have most likely seen pictures of log cabins. The story of log cabins begins with Swedish settlers in 1638. When the first Swedes landed in America, they built houses that were like those in Sweden. They fit together logs that had notched ends. They used clay or moss to fill in any spaces. Then they added a roof. These log houses were snug during cold winters and wet springs.

Read the paragraph. Circle the sentence that tells the main idea. Cross out the sentence that does NOT tell about the main idea.

The United States holds many geography records. The world's largest underground lake is in Tennessee. The world's largest canyon is in Arizona. The deepest canyon in the world is between Idaho and Oregon. The first night baseball game took place in Ohio in 1935. The wettest place in the world is in Hawaii. And Utah has the world's longest natural bridge.

Name_____   **Date**_____

Read the paragraph. Circle the sentence that tells the main idea. Then write a title that tells the main idea.

_____
Title

Bats sleep upside down. They use their wings as blankets when they sleep. A fox curls up in a furry ball and uses its bushy tail as a pillow. Turtles head for the muddy bottom of a pond to doze. For a nap, horses and elephants like to stand up. Birds have special muscles in their legs. That way they can sleep standing on a branch and not fall off. Animals have many different ways of sleeping.

Read the paragraph. Circle the sentence that tells the main idea. Then write a title that tells the main idea.

_____
Title

Three is an important number in many traditional stories. Most likely you have read "The Three Little Pigs." You probably also know the story "Goldilocks and the Three Bears." Some tales are about two brothers or sisters. In many stories a young man has to do three tasks to win a princess. In other tales, such as "The Fisherman and His Wife," the main character is granted three wishes.

Student Record Sheet

Name_____ Date_____

Date	Practice Page # ____	Number Correct	Comments

Answers

☆ ☆ ☆

Page 5:
1. dolphins
2. they learn to play games.
3. they learn to do tricks.
4. tell more about it.
5. first

Page 8:
1. A. detail
   B. main idea
   C. detail

2. A. main idea
   B. detail
   C. detail

3. A. detail
   B. detail
   C. main idea

4. A. main idea
   B. detail
   C. detail

Page 9:
1. A
2. B
3. C

Page 10:
1. C
2. A
3. B

Page 11:
1. B
2. A
3. C

Page 12:
1. C
2. C
3. A

Page 13:
1. C
2. C
3. B

Page 14:
1. A
2. A
3. C

Page 15:
1. C
2. A
3. C

Page 16:
1. A
2. A
3. A

Page 17:
1. B
2. B
3. B

Page 18:
1. C
2. A
3. C

Page 19:
1. B
2. B
3. A

Page 20:
1. C
2. A
3. C

Page 21:
1. A
2. B
3. C

Page 22:
1. B
2. A
3. A

Page 23:
1. C
2. C
3. B

Page 24:
1. B
2. A
3. B

Page 25:
1. B
2. B
3. C

Page 26:
1. B
2. A
3. C

Page 27:
1. A
2. C
3. C

Page 28:
1. A
2. A
3. B

Page 29:
1. C
2. A
3. A

Page 30:
1. C
2. B
3. A

Page 31:
1. A
2. B
3. B

Page 32:
1. B
2. C
3. A

Page 33:
1. C
2. B
3. C

Page 34:
1. A
2. B
3. A

Page 35:
1. C
2. B
3. B

Page 36:
1. A
2. C
3. A

Page 37:
1. C
2. C
3. C

Page 38:
1. B
2. C
3. B

Page 39:
1. B
2. C
3. C

Page 40:
1. A
2. A
3. B

Page 41:
1. C
2. B
3. A

Page 42:
1. B
2. C
3. A

Page 43:
1. A
2. C
3. B

Page 44:
1. Pens have come a long way over time. Possible title: A History of Pens

2. People use many slang terms when they talk about money. Cross out: A lot of people use credit cards instead of cash.

Page 45:
1. The story of log cabins begins with Swedish settlers in 1638. Possible title: The Story of Log Cabins

2. The United States holds many geography records. Cross out: The first night baseball game took place in Ohio in 1935.

Page 46:
1. Animals have many different ways of sleeping. Possible title: How Animals Sleep

2. Three is an important number in many traditional stories. Cross out: Some tales are about two brothers or sisters.